Foreword

This booklet "The story of Ryukyu Kingdom" is a compact Ryukyu history manual published for children, who will be the leaders of our future, with the intention of not letting the facts related to the history of the Ryukyu Kingdom get lost and fade away.

Okinawa is a part of the Nansei archipelago stretching south from Honshu, and was originally an independent nation which used to prosper due to active trade since ancient times. Furthermore, taking advantage of its location, it went through a period of active development as a trading country named "Ryukyu". It is no exaggeration to say that with the help of such circumstances and environment the country could achieve development results that are unique compared with the rest of the world, such as a rich culture comprising of various customs, festivals, and other traditional events.

However, after having been tossed about by the natural flow of different historic events for about 500 years, the history of the Ryukyu Kingdom ended in 1875.

Rather than discussing whether it was good or not, all things that have been created or happened over the years are regarded as "true history", and in order not to let them fade away, I think the existence of a booklet like this one is indispensable.

Certainly, many books and materials dedicated to the history of Ryukyu Kingdom have been published so far. However, I think most of them resemble explanatory booklets and research papers that describe theory.

I am proud to say that this book " The story of Ryukyu Kingdom" is a booklet that offers value as a fun and enjoyable Ryukyu history guidebook that is completely different from various academic books.

The text is structured as straightforward as possible, and the design full with illustrations and figures allows everyone from small children to the elderly to easily read it. Therefore, I hope that this booklet will be used as a simple history textbook that has elements of supplementary reading materials.

Author of Ryukyu picture books
Teruya Tadashi

The beginning of the Ryukyu dynasties …

During the period from approximately 750 to 150 years ago,

Okinawa was once a kingdom of its own. According to some documents,

the first king, King Tenson, came into being soon after the Gusuku castle

building era started following the primitive age.

Dynasties of the Ryukyu Kingdom were the Shunten Dynasty, Eiso Dynasty,

Satto Dynasty, First Sho and Second Sho Dynasties.

It's most likely that the typical history of the Ryukyu Kingdom, which you

might have previously heard of, is that of the Second Sho Dynasty.

An important point when learning history is to understand how the changes

from one dynasty to the next one took place. Let's travel through time together

to the era when Okinawa was once the Ryukyu kingdom.

Table of contents

Shunten Dynasty Period

1187~1260

Story of the First King

The first king, Shunten (Sonton), was the aji (lord) of Urasoe before he became king. In 1187, Sonton became the first king at the age of 20 after defeating the usurper Riyu, who overthrew the Tenson clan which lasted for 25 generations.

His father was Minamoto no Tametomo, and his mother is said to have been the sister of the aji of Ozato. Minamoto no Tametomo left his fate to the deities when he was caught in a storm while he was at sea and drifted to a beach in the northern part of the island of Okinawa. The place at which he arrived was later named "Unten." Soon he met the sister of the aji of Ozato, and Sonton was born.

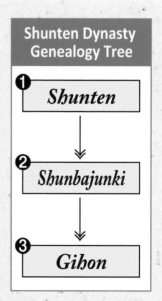

Shunten Dynasty Genealogy Tree

❶ **Shunten**

⬇

❷ **Shunbajunki**

⬇

❸ **Gihon**

The characteristics of this period

An Interesting Legend!

- Hiragana was first introduced as the official written language.
- Population started to have the consciousness of a nation.
- Development of society around the area of Chuzan (in the center of the island of Okinawa).
- There were many natural disasters.
- Infectious diseases were prevalent.
- Farmlands were developed.

Reason for the dynasty change

After the third king Gihon took the throne, the people of Ryukyu were often suffering from hunger and epidemics. In the course of such events, Gihon was concerned that the worsening conditions of his country were brought about due to his lack of virtue. At one point, he called out to Eiso who was said to be a man of virtuous deeds and who was the eldest son of the Lord Eso, the aji of Urasoe, and talked about assigning the throne to him. The country gradually became rich and plentiful from then on. After seven years had passed King Gihon admitted that he himself had less virtue than Eiso and officially assigned the throne to him.

The Kamakura

Eiso Dynasty Period

1260～1350

Story of the First King

It said that Eiso's father, Lord Eso, was a descendant of the Tenson clan. Eiso's mother had a dream that before she became pregnant, the Sun came down close to her and entered her stomach. It is also said that the room she was in was filled by beautiful light which rose up to white clouds in the sky when Eiso was born. Because of that, King Eiso was thereafter named "the child of the Sun".

Eiso Dynasty Genealogy Tree

❶ *Eiso*

❷ *Taisei*

❸ *Eiji*

❹ *Tamagusuku*

❺ *Seii*

The characteristics of this period

An Interesting Legend!

- Farmland was equally divided for the ease of agriculture.
- The kingdom's land was clearly subdivided into villages.
- The monk Zenkan arrived to Okinawa.
- Temples started to be built.
- The Yōdore royal mausoleum was created.
- The system of tributary goods was started.

Reason for the dynasty change

Due to the fact that the dynasty's fourth king, Tamagusuku, was conducting the kingdom's politics negligently, several ajis abandoned their loyalty and began controlling each one of their areas independently causing the country to divide into three parts. Meanwhile in Chuzan, Seii was enthroned at the age of ten as the fifth king, however his mother was actually the one controlling the country's politics. After king Seii died, the eldest son who took over was only five years old, so the aji of Urasoe named Satto was recommended as the king by senior officials because of his vast popularity.

Next Page →

Period		The Muromachi Period
		1336

Satto Dynasty Period

1350〜1405

Story of the First King

Satto's father was said to be a farmer and his mother a heavenly nymph. Satto, who possessed mysterious charm, was able to marry the daughter of aji of Katsuren. When she married him and came to his house, all the utensils in the kitchen turned into gold. Satto then sold it for money and bought farming tools that were given out to poor farmers. Because of that Satto received support from farmers and became the aji of Urasoe.

Satto Dynasty Genealogy Tree

❶ **Satto**

❷ **Bunei**

The characteristics of this period

An Interesting Legend!

- Characters in the name of the country were changed from 流求 to 琉球.
- Study journeys to China began.
- 36 families from China naturalized in Kume.
- King Bunei welcomed the Chinese emissary for the first time. at his enthronement ceremony in 1403.

Reason for the dynasty change

After his enthronement, King Satto's son Bunei, after the enthronement, started running the country for his own convenience and benefit. During that time, the aji of Sashiki named Hashi sent the King a harsh letter of criticism causing a conflict to begin. Hashi who held the trust of ajis from the Chuzan region allied with them and took control the area. Next, he conquered Hokuzan、Nanzan and unified them into Sanzan. However, due to various reasons, his father Shisho was enthroned as the King.

After that, Hashi sent an emissary to China to report about his activities. Chinese emissaries visited in return and acknowledged Shisho as the King of Ryukyu. As a token of commemoration China gave the new dynasty the name "Sho". That was the beginning of the First Sho dynasty.

The Muromachi

First Sho Dynasty Period

1402～1466

Story of the First King

The dynasty's first king Shoshisho started from them. Shoshisho's father was born on Iheiya island. Then he moved to Izena island and practiced agriculture for a living. He soon became a wealthy land owner and was envied by the inhabitants of the island due to which he had to flee the island. After his departure he arrived at the beach in Sashiki. There he met the aji of Oshiro. The aji had his daughter marry the father of Shoshisho as he was told to do so by a god in his dream. The dynasty's first king Shoshisho was born to them.

First Sho Dynasty Genealogy Tree

❶ **Shoshisho**
❷ **Shohashi**
❸ **Shochu**
❹ **Shoshitatsu**
❺ **Shokinpuku**
❻ **Shotaikyu**
❼ **Shotoku**

The characteristics of this period

An Interesting Legend!

- Land reclamation works were performed to link Shuri and Naha (The Chōkōtei Road).
- All three regions on the main island (Sanzan) were unified in 1429.
- Shuri castle was significantly rebuilt and expanded.
- The Ryutan pond was created.
- Naha port was enlarged.
- The dynasty name "Sho" was granted by China's Xuande Emperor.

Reason for the dynasty change

The 7th king, Shotoku, was a person of brilliant intelligence but he was also selfish. Kanamaru, who was a senior statesman during Shotoku's reign couldn't stand Shotoku's ways of doing things and left the castle. The next year, after Shotoku died, there was a discussion about who should be the next king. A gray-haired old man appeared and started to criticize what Shotoku had done while occupying the throne. Then he told the senior statesmen that it was the time to elect a new king from among ordinary people instead of letting Shotoku's son inherit the throne and that Kanamaru was the person. They unanimously agreed with the old man. At that time, Kanamaru was in Uchima in the city of Nishihara. He had withdrawn from public life. The senior statesmen persuaded Kanamaru to be the king and finally he agreed. That was the rise of King Shoen, previously known as Uchima Kanamaru.

Next Page

Period

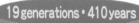
Second Sho Dynasty Period

Story of the First King

Uchima Kanamaru, later known as Shoen was born to a farmer on the island of Izena. His ancestors were from outside of the island, so he started to be envied by the natives of the island after he had success in being a farmer. Due to that he moved to Kunigami Village. After that he moved to Shuri. Shotaikyu (the oji (prince) of Goeku) knew Kanamaru's situation so he invited Kanamaru to Goeku castle. After Shotaikyu acceded to the throne, Kanamaru became a senior statesman. Then, during the reign of Shotoku, the state affairs were in turmoil, and Kanamaru, who had many distinguished achievements, ascended the throne.

The characteristics of this period

- Tamaudun, the mausoleum for successive generations of the Second Sho dynasty was built.
- The Shureimon Gate of Shuri Castle was built.
- People were made to lay down weapons, and all ajis were gathered in Shuri.
- "Edo nobori", missions of gratitude and celebrations to Edo, the capital of Tokugawa Japan, were started.
- Shuri Castle was surrendered.
- Improvements in performing arts, culture, and education.

Second Sho Dynasty Genealogy Trees

1 Shoen
2 Shoseni
3 Shoshin
4 Shosei
5 Shogen
6 Shoei
7 Shonei
8 Shobou
9 Shoken
10 Shoshitsu
11 Shotei
12 Shoeki
13 Shokei
14 Shoboku
15 Shoon
16 Shosei
17 Shoko
18 Shoiku
19 Shotai

The Muromachi Period	The Azuchi-Momoyama period	
	1568	1603

Invasion by Satsuma

The Shimazu clan (Satsuma), who had been strengthening control over the trade in Ryukyu since the second half of the 16th century, gradually came to treat Ryukyu with heightening pressure, and continued to crack down on the country. On the grounds of their worsening financial situation, on February 26, 1609 Satsuma decided to start the invasion of Ryukyu. 19 new laws were enacted and the invasion was ordered. Shonei, the Ryukyu king of the time, offered to enter talks with the Satsuma shoguns in an attempt to prevent the invasion. They made it a condition that they would hold senior statesmen, such as royal family members and three ministers, in Satsuma as hostages. The king couldn't make such a decision and come to an agreement and as a result, Ryukyu ended up surrendering Shuri castle to Satsuma on April 5th, 1609. From then on Ryukyu ended up completely under Satsuma's control.

Sad event!

The Dawn of a New Era

In 1872 (year 5 of the Meiji era) the 19th king, Shotai, and two other officials received an order to appear at the Japanese government. The Japanese government wanted to define the status of Ryukyu. Though Ryukyu had been under the domination of Satsuma for about 300 years, it was also recognized as a country when trading with the Qing dynasty (China) and other countries. The reason why the Japanese government took this action was a problem with Taiwan which happened a year earlier. Japan was able to defend its stance against the Qing dynasty and the Japanese government then recognized Ryukyu as a prefecture of Japan and not a vassal state of Qing. In 1874, "the abolition of the han system and establishment of prefectures" brought an end to the history of the Ryukyu Kingdom. The last king, Shotai, moved to Tokyo and spent the rest of his life there.

The Origin of Name of Ryukyu

It is said that the origin of the name of Ryukyu dates back to about 650 years ago. Ono no Imoko (the person who went in China as an envoy to the Sui Dynasty) once explained to envoys from China that Okinawa was called the land of 'Iyakukunijin'. When envoys from China returned to their home country, they used the word 流求, which is read as "Ryukyu" to describe the islands. Then in 1372, the word 琉球 started to be used more commonly because people thought 琉球 looks more beautiful than 流求. This is how the name of the country Ryukyu came into existence.

To the present

The Edo Period

World Heritage

The Nine World Heritage sites of Okinawa

**"The Gusuku Sites and Related Properties of the Kingdom of Ryukyu"
was registered as UNESCO World Heritage site in December 2000.**

In November 2000, the UNESCO's 24th World Heritage Committee meeting was held, and on December 2, 2000 "The Gusuku Sites and Related Properties of the Kingdom of Ryukyu" (consisting of 9 sites) was officially registered as Japan's 11th World Heritage site. The indigenous Ryukyu masonry construction examples such as Nakijin Castle Ruins located in the northern part of Okinawa, and the sacred place Seifa-Utaki, both representing the indigenous religion and culture of Ryukyu which are still handed down from generation to generation, were recognized as world treasures.
These World Heritage sites are scattered throughout the northern, central, and southern regions of Okinawa and add a lot to attractiveness of tourism on the island.

The Nine World Heritage
sites of Okinawa

World heritage

Nakijin Castle Ruins

The residence castle of the king of Hokuzan, a prominent man in the northern region during the Sanzan period.

Nakijin castle was built on top of a hill at the height of 100 meters above the sea level. The beautifully curved masonry ramparts extend to the length of 1,500m. Lord Hananchi was the last who resided at the castle. He was overthrown by King Shohashi in 1416.

Nakijin Castle Ruins

Location / Nakijinson Imadomari 5101
Phone / 0980-56-4400

★Nakijin Castle Ruins

Imadomari Intersection

Hokuzan High School

Nakaoji Intersection

Nago→

●Hokuzan Supermarket

Kaneku→

Haneji Inland Sea

Head north from Naha Airport to Nago City. Turn left at the Nakaoji intersection and drive for about 10 km. The site will be on the left.

553081414*44

Please input this map code into your car navigation system to be guided to the location.

Zakimi Castle Ruins

The castle that had the most significance as a military fortress during the Ryukyu dynasty.

Zakimi Castle was constructed in the early 15th century by Gosamaru. It is highly valued for the beautiful curves of its Aikata masonry ramparts. Wedge stones, which are a distinctive characteristic of the castle, are inserted into the two arch gates.

Zakimi Castle Ruins ★Zakimi Castle Ruins

Location / Yomitan Zakimi 70□□ — Pay attention to the signboard!
Phone / 098-958-3141

Takashiho intersection — Iramina intersection

Yomitan High School

Cape Zanpa

Yomitan Post Office
JA Yomitan
Yomitan Gas Center

Ryukyu Bank
Yomitan Branch

Docomo
Shop
Yomitan
Branch

Murasakimura

Head north on Route 58 towards Nago and turn left at the Yomitan Village Iramina intersection. Proceed for about 7 km from there and turn right at the Takashiho intersection. After about 4 minutes, turn left. The site is about 50 m ahead on the right.

33854428*55

Please input this map code into your car navigation system to be guided to the location.

Katsuren Castle Ruins

An old castle built in a scenic spot on a steep rocky mountain.

Katsuren Castle was built on a hill on top of a precipitous cliff, 100m above sea level. The construction date is unknown. The last lord of the castle was Amawari, who was its 10th lord. Around that time, overseas trade was flourishing, and Katsuren Castle is said to have flourished the most.

Katsuren Castle Ruins

Location / 3807-2 Katsurenhaebaru, Uruma City
Phone / 098-978-7373

Yokatsu Intersection

Okinawa Electric
Power Yokatsu Substation

Yokatsu Junior High School

Shioya Intersection

Katsuren Castle Ruins

Toyo Apartments

Sugar Factory

Go north on Uruma City Prefectural Road 85 towards Katsuren and turn right at the Shioya intersection. The site will be on the right side after you drive for about 3 km.

mt 499570239*52

Please input this map code
into your car navigation system
to be guided to the location.

Nakagusuku Castle Ruins

▌ The castle of the famous shogun "Gosamaru" from the era when many battles took place.

Nakagusuku Castle was built in the early 15th century by King Sho Taikyu. The beauty of the castle is admired in a book titled "Narrative of the Expedition of an American Squadron to the China Seas and Japan," which was published by Commodore Perry who visited Okinawa in 1853.

Nakagusuku Castle Ruins

Location / Kitanakagusukuson
Ogusuku 503
Phone / 098-935-5719

U.S. military base

←Legion Club

Toguchi intersection→

Adaniya intersection

Okinawa Expressway Kitanakagusuku Interchange

Nakamura Family Residence●

Nishihara→

Nakagusuku Castle Ruins ★

Nishihara→

From Naha Airport, head north on the Okinawa Expressway, get off at the Kitanakagusuku Interchange, turn right and exit on National Highway 146. Follow the road toward the Toguchi intersection and turn right towards the "Nakamura Family Residence". The site will be on the right side after you drive for about 2 km.

33411769*41

Please input this map code into your car navigation system to be guided to the location.

Shurijo Castle Ruins

※Photographed in 2015, before Shuri Castle burned down

A castle that symbolizes the splendor of the Ryukyu dynasty.

Shurijo Castle is where the Ryukyu Kingdom ended. It was the center of Ryukyu politics, economy, and culture until the abolishment of the feudal domain system and the introduction of the prefectural system in 1879. It burned down completely during the Battle of Okinawa, but was restored in 1992 before burning down again in 2019.

Shuri Castle Ruins

Location / 1-2 Shurikinjocho, Naha City
Phone / 098-886-2020

Shuri Castle Ruins ★

Tamaudun

Sonohyan-utaki Ishimon

Shureimon Gate

From Naha Airport, head north toward Nago and turn right at the Izumizaki rotary intersection. From there, go through Kokusai-dori and turn right at the end of the street. Head towards Shuri. The castle will be on the right after you travel for about 2.3km.

MAPCODE 33161497*55

Please input this map code into your car navigation system to be guided to the location.

Sonohyan-utaki Ishimon

█ It is a stone gate that also served as a sacred place for prayers for the peace and prosperity of the nation.

The stone gate was built during the reign of King Shoshin in 1591 by a mason from Taketomi Island named Nishito. Whenever the king left the castle on a journey, he would stop by at the gate to pray for safe travels.

Sonohyan-utaki Ishimon

Location: 1-7 Shurimawashicho, Naha City
Phone / 098-886-2020

Sonohyan-utaki Ishimon

Tera↑

Restaurants and shops
in Shurijo Castle Park

Shurijo Castle Park Management Center

From Naha Airport, head north toward Nago and turn right at the Izumizaki rotary intersection. From there, go through Kokusai-dori and turn right at the end of the street. Head toward Shuri. The site is adjacent to the northwest side of Shuri Castle which will be on the right side after traveling about 2.3km.

`33161639*65`

Please input this map code into your car navigation system to be guided to the location.

Tamaudun

▍ Ryukyu's unique mausoleum where the kings of the Second Sho dynasty era were laid to rest.

Tamaudun was built in 1501 by King Shoshin as the royal mausoleum for the Ryukyu Kingdom to rebury his father King Shoen. Even now in modern Japan, this unique mausoleum, indigenous to the Ryukyus, is regarded as an important stone-made monument.

Tamaudun

Location / 1-3, Shurikinjocho, Naha City
Phone / 098-885-2861

P

P

Shuri Castle Park

Tempura shop

Tamaudun
★

English school

Kannon Temple

Shuri High School

From Naha Airport, head north toward Nago and turn right at the Izumizaki rotary intersection. From there, go through Kokusai-dori and turn right at the end of the street. Head toward Shuri. The site is located to the west of Shuri Castle which will be on the right side after traveling about 2.3km.

33160659*77

Please input this map code
Into your car navigation system
to be guided to the location.

Shikinaen

A park with a mixture of Chinese and Japanese garden styles in which visitors were warmly welcomed.

Shikinaen gardens and palace were built to welcome and entertain envoys from China. It was also a place of the second residence of the royal families. It is said that Chinese envoys admired this unique Ryukyu-style garden, in which both Japanese and Chinese styles are intertwined.

Shikinaen

Location / 421-7 Maaji, Naha City
Phone / 098-855-5936

'Inaka' Restaurant
Maaji Public Hall
Shikina Reien
Imai pan
Ryukyu Shikinain
Shuri
Asahibashi
Ichahanbashi
Arakawa intersection
Yonabaru
★Shikinaen

Head north from Naha Airport towards Nago. Turn right at the Asahibashi intersection and drive for about 5km toward Yonabaru. Turn left at the Kamima intersection, go up the slope and turn left at the Arakawa intersection. After 50 meters, climb the overpass on the left hand side and proceed for about 1 km, the site will be on the left side.

33130089*45

Please input this map code into your car navigation system to be guided to the location.

Seifa-Utaki

A worship spot facing Kudaka Island, "the Island of Gods". It was also the most important sacred place in the Ryukyu Kingdom.

Seifa-Utaki is located in the southern part of Okinawa Island. It is a sacred place where Amamikiyo, the founding god of the Ryukyu Islands, is said to have descended to Earth. There are six sanctuaries called "Ibi," and the names of three of them, "Ufugui," "Yuinchi," and "Sangui," are the same as the names for rooms at the Shuri Castle.

Seifa Utaki

Location / 539 Kudeken, Chinen, Nanjo City
Phone / 098-949-1899

★Seifa Utaki

Manmaru Cafe●

●Chinen Post Office

●Azama Sun Sun Beach

←Tamagusuku

●Ganju Station
●Cape Chinen Park

Head north for Nago from Naha Airport. Turn right at the Asahibashi intersection and go straight for about 10 km. Go straight through the Yonabaru intersection and travel for about 14 km toward Chinen in Nanjo City. The site will be on the right side after passing Cape Chinen.

[mt] 232594734*71

Please input this map code into your car navigation system to be guided to the location.

The Story of Ryukyu Kingdom

Three important stories

During the Ryukyu dynasties era, which lasted about 450 years various important events took place.
Here will introduce three stories that can be said to be the most representative among those events.
Because of such significant historical events the Ryukyu kingdom was able to develop until the dynasty era ended.

Sanzan unification

By the beginning of the 15th century, the three small kingdoms, Hokuzan, Chuzan, and Nanzan, were heading toward unification. At that time, Sho Hashi, who was the aji of Sashiki, which belonged to Nanzan, defeated King Bunei of Urasoe and took over the Chuzan Kingdom. Furthermore, Nakijin Castle that dominated over the Hokuzan area and Osato Castle belonging to the Nanzan area were attacked and destroyed, and as a result, the three kingdoms were successfully unified in 1429.

After the unification of Sanzan (three kingdoms), Sho Hashi, who became the king, started the First Sho dynasty and laid the foundation for future generations. However, the power of the local aji was still strong, and a completely centralized government couldn't be formed even after that. The dynasty's administration did not last long, and the royal family ended on its 7th generation after 64 years of reign.

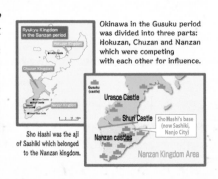

Okinawa in the Gusuku period was divided into three parts: Hokuzan, Chuzan and Nanzan which were competing with each other for influence.

Sho Hashi was the aji of Sashiki which belonged to the Nanzan kingdom.

Ryukyu Kingdom in the Sanzan period

Hokuzan Kingdom

Chuzan Kingdom

Nanzan Kingdom

Gusuku (castle)

Urasoe Castle

Shuri Castle

Sho Hashi's base (now Sashiki, Nanjo City)

Nanzan castles

Nanzan Kingdom Area

20

Invasion of Ryukyu by Satsuma (being under the control of Satsuma domain)

In the beginning of 17th century, the Shimazu clan of Satsuma domain landed at Unten Port in the northern part of the main island of Okinawa in 1609, and first attacked Nakijin Castle. After that, the Satsuma army went south and laid siege to Shuri.

The circumstances in Ryukyu around that time were not very favorable, and trade with neighboring countries, which was one of the centers of the economy, gradually withered and with it the kingdom's power was also declining. Therefore, Shuri Castle fell without resistance by the Ryukyuan army. King Sho Nei decided to surrender Shuri Castle and withdrew from it.

The Ryukyu Kingdom, whose main economic pillar was trade with southern countries such as China, saw its politics and society gradually change after the invasion by Satsuma as taxes were forcefully levied and profits from China trade were taken away.

Disposition of Ryukyu (The abolition of the han (domains) system)

In 1875 (8th year of Meiji era), the Meiji government decided to dispose of "Ryukyu" and enforced its policy. The government urged the Ryukyu Domain to dismantle the Ryukyu kingdom system and to replace it by Okinawa Prefecture belonging to Japan. In the same year, it dispatched Michiyuki Matsuda as the disposition officer, and issued the following four orders.

1. To abolish the envoy exchange and tributary relationship with the Qing dynasty and cut ties with China.
2. To commission young officials to study the new system and sciences.
3. To reform the political system in line with other prefectures of Japan.
4. To set up a garrison branch (military facility) to implement these reforms without disorder.

Based on this order, the Ryukyu Domain disappeared in 1879. It was decided that Ryukyu was to belong to Japan. The Ryukyu Kingdom, which lasted for about 450 years, came to an end.

Disposition officer
Michiyuki Matsuda

Traditional crafts

There is a wide variety of traditional crafts that appeared and were developing during the Ryukyu dynasty period. Among them, the bingata textile dyeing art, which has been influenced by Chinese calico textile and has its own path of development, is a unique craft that has been unmatched even worldwide. It has been attracting attention from the viewpoint of folkloristics due to its unique techniques and beauty for about 100 years. Here we will give you an introduction of typical traditional crafts such as ceramics, lacquer ware, sanshin, etc.

Ceramics

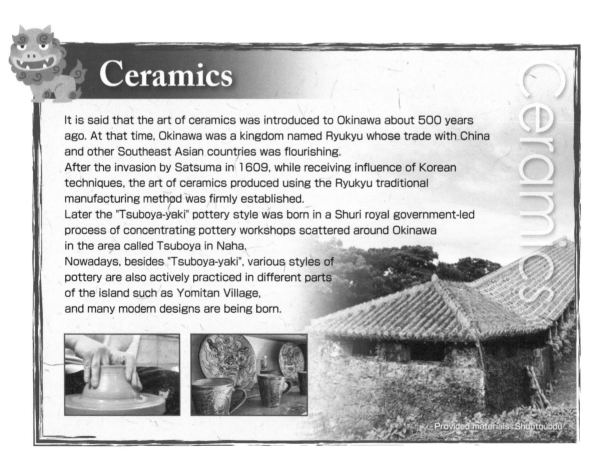

It is said that the art of ceramics was introduced to Okinawa about 500 years ago. At that time, Okinawa was a kingdom named Ryukyu whose trade with China and other Southeast Asian countries was flourishing.

After the invasion by Satsuma in 1609, while receiving influence of Korean techniques, the art of ceramics produced using the Ryukyu traditional manufacturing method was firmly established.

Later the "Tsuboya-yaki" pottery style was born in a Shuri royal government-led process of concentrating pottery workshops scattered around Okinawa in the area called Tsuboya in Naha.

Nowadays, besides "Tsuboya-yaki", various styles of pottery are also actively practiced in different parts of the island such as Yomitan Village, and many modern designs are being born.

Provided materials : Shubtoubou

Dyed fabrics

Trade with China and Southeast Asia was flourishing
from 14th until 16th centuries and the Ryukyu Kingdom prospered.
It is said that the products of dyeing and weaving techniques
were typical goods for trade.
In particular, dyed products has been influenced by the Chinese calico
and Japanese yuzen styles and developed as a Ryukyu traditional style.
It is undeniable that the development of the art of dyeing
and weaving was protected by the Shuri royal government,
but "bingata" is a craft that is highly valued worldwide
and is recognized in the field of folkloristics.
Okinawa's dyeing and weaving techniques
will continue to be refined which will lead
to even more beautiful and attractive items
appearing in the future.

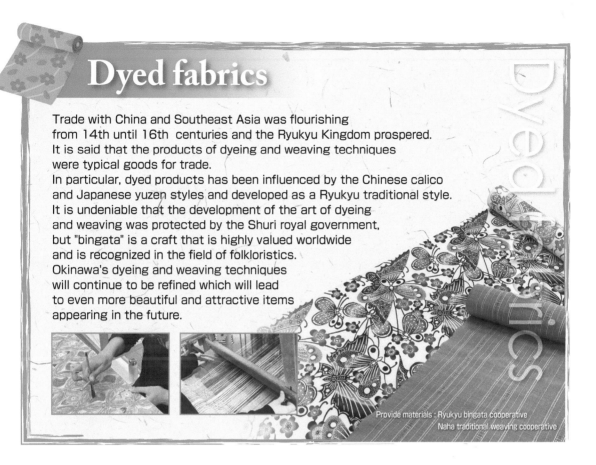

Provide materials : Ryukyu bingata cooperative
Naha traditional weaving cooperative

Lacquerware

It is said that lacquerware techniques were introduced
to Okinawa from China around 14th and 15th centuries.
Since lacquerware production in the latter half
of the 16th century was under the control of the
Ryukyu government, craftsmen were required to improve
their skills and level of production.
In the 18th century, when the golden
age of Ryukyu lacquerware began,
many decorative techniques were born.
One of the most representative of them is the
decoration technique called
"Tsuikin". Ryukyu lacquerware products
were much valued as gifts to the emperor of
China and to the shogun of Edo.
The "Ryukyu lacquerware" inherited from
the Ryukyu dynasty continues

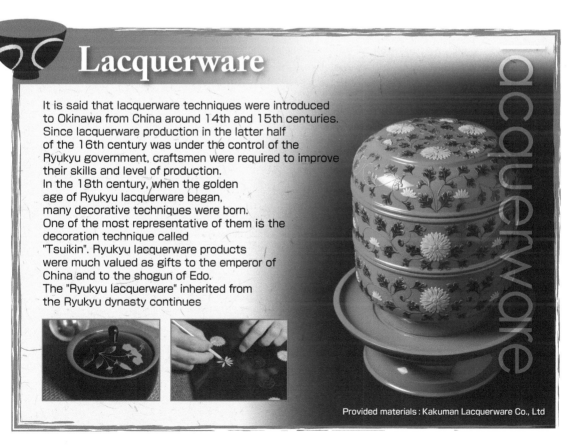

Provided materials : Kakuman Lacquerware Co., Ltd

Sanshin

It is said that the sanshin was introduced to Ryukyu around
the end of the 14th century. Legend has it that the predecessor
to sanshin was brought by 36 migrants
from China who moved to Kume in Naha City.
After that, through repeated improvements it evolved into modern sanshin.
Sanshin is an indispensable musical instrument
in traditional Okinawan performing arts,
and is widely used in Ryukyuan dance,
"Kumi Odori", folk songs, "Eisa", etc. In recent years,
it has become popular in the music industry
as it has been increasingly used in popular songs and music.
Its familiar and unadorned tone makes
it an instrument that captivates people's hearts.

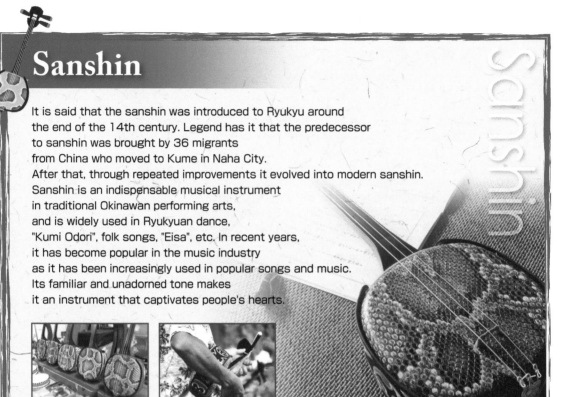

●References   Ryukyu Kingdom Secret Story (Warabe Shobo)
             Understand the Ryukyu Kingdom! (Seibido Shuppan)
             Okinawan traditional crafts (Okinawa Bunkasha)
             Illustrations - Ryukyu Traditional Crafts (Kawade Shobo Shinsha)
             Fascinated by the old sanshin (Border Ink)
●Cooperation Naha City Museum of History
●Cover design Teruya Tadashi

Enjoy slipping in time into the Ryukyu dynasties period

The story of Ryukyu Kingdom

First edition published   October 19, 2022
Edited by Teruya Tadashi
Published by Teruya Tadashi
Publisher Ryukyu Kikaku
English translation Maksim Lobatyy
        Japan, 902-0064
        3-7-36-3F Yosemiya, Naha City, Okinawa Prefecture
        TEL / FAX 098-831-6349 Mobile 090-7586-0770
        E-mail: taitai2919@gmail.com
        Https://ryukyuhistory.jp/

Ryukyu Planning web site   YouTube   Teruya Tadashi Business website
Shopify shop   base shop